HYPER GROWTH: HOW TO CONNECT TO YOUR CUSTOMERS IN NEW WAYS!

7 Creative Strategies to Capture Your Next Customer, Partner & Investor

Plus, Seven Critical Tools That Every Professional Needs to Get in Front of Anyone

D1557410

**Taimour Zaman Founder,
The Access Group**
www.access-group.ca

The Access Group

Book Orders

Order at Amazon.com. Special discounts are available on quantity purchases by corporations, non-profits, associations, and others. For details, contact the Taimour Zaman at taimour@access-group.ca

Charity

A portion of book proceeds will be donated to orphans in India: Jan Madhyam.
This is dedicated to Jaleh Namazie.

Keynote Speeches and Press Interviews

For keynote speeches and press interviews, please contact the author at taimour@access-group.ca

Royalties for Book Translations

To earn royalties from translating this book into any language, please contact the publisher at taimour@access-group.ca

ISBN: 978-1-77277-184-8

Taimour's clients have said...

"Taimour's passion, energy, and commitment to Innovation are inspirational. He is an innovator when it comes to getting diverse groups of people together to improve Canada's innovation on the global stage."

Ross Pellizzari,
President, Managing Director, Avaya

....

"Taimour is skilled at designing and selling "mission impossible" projects and pulling together the teams to implement. I worked directly with him on the design of several of these initiatives. His unique gift is creativity. He does not think outside the box; he creates something entirely original, new and fresh. His work is transformative. He is skilled at working with multinational corporations, communities of interest, government leaders and innovation agents. He has been involved in projects around job creation, immigration, healthcare, mobile banking, and marketing. His network of contacts is international in scope and second-to-none in depth."

Susan Dineen,
Senior Vice President of Technology,
New Media and Strategic Marketing,
Sony Music Entertainment Canada

....

"I have had the great pleasure to work very closely with Taimour. He is an inspiring innovator with relentless energy and passion. His relationship management skills are second to none. Taimour has developed loyal and dedicated long-term relationships with such a huge multidisciplinary group of professionals at all levels of business, academia and government. He is a creative thinker with unique, and outside-the-box-ideation capabilities. An absolute pleasure to work with"

Jerry Boyer,
CIO, Glaxo Smith Kline

"I have worked with, participated in projects with, sought expertise from and advised Taimour for over a decade. He is one of the most engaged and engaging people on the planet. He is an uncannily effective networker and linker of people and projects. He is the interstices between people and provides great leadership by simply asking lots of questions and listening carefully and thoughtfully to the answers. If I were responsible for a business project that required GREAT socialization to build a sense of purpose, consensus, and community, Taimour would be my first call. He is simply that good."

Bruce Taylor,
EVP, Data Centre Dynamics

Dedication

For my parents, who raised and supported me throughout my life. Special thanks to my father who was one of the most respected and best sales professional that I've ever met and has now passed away.

To Anitra Zaman, with whom everything is possible.

To my dear brother, Shaan Zaman, who is a man of compassion and integrity.

And to my beloved business partner, Sai Mohammad, whose idea was for me to make a contribution to the world by sharing my stories about how I get to meet anybody.

I also want to give a special thanks to my business partners/colleagues at 1 Plus 12 (www.1plus12.com) and the support/training they provide in real estate investments.

Foreword

I am excited to introduce you to Taimour Zaman's book, Hyper Growth: How to Connect to Your Customers in New Ways! Taimour is a world-class lead generation consultant. In his book, he shares his knowledge and experience on how you can leverage new technologies, such as artificial intelligence. He also shares with you many creative techniques to get in front of your customers, investors or business partners, and his advice is second to none.

Hyper Growth is a must read for you. Taimour provides you with real-life examples and case studies in how to get in front of your target audience and sell mission impossible projects to diverse groups of people, with various levels of interest.

I was pleasantly surprised to see so many tactics that could help you exponentially grow your organization by engaging existing communities and busi-ness celebrities. This book will show you how to increase your number of qualified leads, move people faster through your sales cycle and increase your close rates.

I highly recommend this book, and suggest that you implement Taimour's strategies so that you can start connecting to your customers and becoming even more successful!

Raymond Aaron
Success Coach and
New York Times Best Selling Author

Acknowledgements

I want to acknowledge the love of my dear parents and family for showing faith in me.

I couldn't write this book if it weren't for the support of my dear wife Anitra Persad and my business partner Sai Mohammad.

I want to thank Andy Aicklen, Principal of Aicklen & Associates for taking my cold calls and emails.

I especially need to thank Doug Cummings, SVP of Q9 Networks for taking my first-ever cold call and for consistently introducing me to his colleagues and network.

I want to thank Ross Pellizzari for the difference has made in my life and career.

I want to thank Bruce Taylor for being such a great friend, client and supporter.

I want to acknowledge Howard Lichtman for being a supporter of all of my programs and services.

I want to acknowledge Peter Ciceri, CEO Coach and Career Counsellor – whose support and insights have changed the direction of my career.

I want to acknowledge Paul McDevitt and Brantz Myers from Cisco Systems for helping me set up One Million Acts of Person-Centered Health.

I want to thank Wayne Mills, Ted Maulucci and John King for helping me start One Million Acts of Innovation.

I want to thank Don Chapman for his years of coaching and advice.

CHAPTER 1:

How to Design Advisory Boards or Master Minds that leads to New Capital or New Customers

Chapter 1:

How to Design Advisory Boards or Master Minds That Lead Capital or New Customers

"It is a common experience that a problem difficult at night is resolved in the morning after the committee of sleep has worked on it."
– John Steinbeck

Have you ever had a career in a company where you felt bored and under-utilized? I know I have. The year is 1997. I've been awarded the top performing employee in my department at Dell Computers. There's only one problem. I'm bored to death at my job. My manager has no clue what to do with me and I can't see any exciting career opportunities for me.

So, I join a cool networking club hoping to meet a few interesting people and sure enough that is where I meet Zale Tabakman. He's the CEO of a startup company called 3dOnThe.Net and Zale needs help: Everything from strategy to investment funding to capturing new customers. After a few coffee conversations, Zale and I seem to admire each other's skills and that's when Zale asked me to consider putting together an advisory board for him.

Well, the following morning I'm at the coffee shop at the bottom of our office building and it's where I bump into Bruce Melhuish – our Chief Financial Officer. As I started to have a conversation with him, I told him about my side project and asked Bruce to consider joining the board. Given the success Bruce had with previous startups, he was quick to agree to join the board. Having Bruce on board, I started to identify some of Dell's strategic accounts by going to various websites and identifying a few dozen executives in each company. Within three weeks, I had an appointment with Josh Mandelson, Senior Vice President of CIBC; Bruce Derraugh, Vice President at Bell Canada, and few other reputable companies. Shortly after that, 3dOnThe.Net had its first advisory board meeting and secured access to some capital and introductions into a few large enterprise accounts.

I managed to leverage my work on the advisory board to jump into my new career at Bell Canada with a 92% raise in my starting salary.

If what you and your organization require is strategic advice, access to new customers and/or access to capital, I highly recommend putting together advisory boards.

After designing dozens and dozens of powerful advisory boards around the world, here is my blueprint for how to design and facilitate advisory board meetings.

FIRST, identify the outcome of the company/project. Often times this is called the Mission Statement or the Purpose of the Organization or the purpose/mission of the project. It is fundamental to have a purpose that is greater than one's self: A purpose that is big and inspiring. It cannot be about making a million dollars for you, because no one cares about that.

It's rather about how to solve a big problem that the world cares about. If for instance, you have software that is about helping sales people with lead generation, then maybe your bigger than life goal is to help eliminate the frustration of millions of sales people around the world when it comes to lead generation. If you are a lawyer who wants to focus on family law, then maybe the purpose of your organization is how to ensure that kids from divorced families end up having successful lives. The key in putting together an advisory board is to have a noble cause that engages people.

Here are some examples of big ideas:

- Gahndi - India shall be free
- TED - Ideas worth spreading
- Kennedy: a man on the moon by end of the century
- Microsoft: A computer on every desktop.
- Nike: To bring inspiration and innovation to every athlete in the world.
- Apple: A computer in the hands of everyday people.
- Google: To provide access to the world's information in one click.

SECOND is to identify stakeholders for your organization and have a clear purpose of why you are inviting them to take time from their busy schedules to participate in this program with you.

THIRD, when inviting stakeholders to participate, you always want to ask them what it is that they see in this program for themselves.

Warning: if you come across someone who is clearly only looking out for their financial well-being, reconsider inviting them to participate. Your core values and the things you care about (example – making sure kids from divorced couples have a successful future) must align with the core values of the advisors you are bringing on board. If you don't have your values aligned, keep searching until you find the right person.

FOURTH, clearly communicate your advisory board dates, times and locations so that people know what their commitments are.

FIFTH, include relationship-building exercises as part of the agenda so that people feel safe in sharing their knowledge and expertise. This will dramatically help you produce unimaginable results.

SIXTH, when presenting your big idea, questions, etc., you need to be able to speak to people who learn differently. In my presentations, we always start with why, what, how, and what if.

Some people are all about the why and as long as the why has been answered, they are good to go. Some others are all about the what. They need to know what this is about, what it will accomplish and for whom? Some people are all about the how: how are we going to do this and who is going to do what. Some people are about mismanagement and care about "what if this goes wrong". Having these answers prepared ahead of time will help you engage your target audience much faster.

During my work with Zale Tabakman, he introduced me to Rick Wolfe and Alan Kay. Both are independent consultants who have a long working relationship with each other and are both expert facilitators. I spent about five years of my career working with these 2 individuals learning the art of complex group facilitation. That is when I started my own consulting company – The Access Group. Its mission is to connect sales people with new prospective customers. Sales and Marketing executives would hire me for $20,000-$45,000 per event and my job was to fill up the room with hundreds of their strategic customers and help them kick start their sales process.

In the next chapter, I will share new techniques in cold calling. You will start to see how cold calling will never disappear (in a digital world) and how it will take a new shape in the 21st century.

CHAPTER 2:

Cold Calling

Chapter 2:

Why Cold Calling Will Never Die and How to do it Correctly

"It is the cold that is dead – not the calling."
- Trish Bertuzzi, CEO and Chief Strategist of The Bridge Group Inc.

When I started my event business (The Access Group) I needed sponsors (companies that would fund my events). I needed to cold call potential companies that were interested in sponsoring the themes of my events and I needed to be good at getting them to sign up as a sponsor.

My first call was to Joanne Moretti, the GM of Computer Associates (CA). I left her a voicemail asking her if she could sponsor my breakfast session. The following day, her director of marketing contacted me and gave me the funding

I was looking for. Later that year, Media Live International decided to hire me for my ability to recruit executives into their conferences. Their primary target was financial institutions. I went online looking for names of executives in Canadian financial services and I cold called the top 7 senior executives. A few days after, I received a call from Jim Rager's office. Jim at the time was the vice chairman of RBC – the largest bank in Canada. Years after, when I was building my first global platform, I called a technology association looking for corporate sponsors. The technology association referred me to someone called Bob (Robert) Lane. Bob is Steve Jobs former colleague from Pixar. I never knew who Bob was when I cold-called him. Bob and I have now done a few events together, spoken at conferences together and I consider him one of the best people in the world that I've cold called in my life – ever.

My conclusion – cold calling isn't dead. Humans are wired to be connected with each other. And digital platforms (like Facebook) will strengthen the connection for folks who are far away from each other.

And as digital platforms become smarter and busier in terms of content, cold calling will take a new shape.

For instance, if you are an author of a book, you may want to identify key influencers on Twitter for your subject matter and "cold call" them to see if you can create a partnership with them.

Here are the lessons I've learned from cold calling executives:

To be effective at cold calling, you need to have a compelling story that truly excites you. That is one reason why hiring call centers to set up appointments (in my opinion) doesn't work. Outsourced agents don't have the passion that you have and can't relay that passion on your behalf on the telephone.

You also need to know that when you are cold calling someone, you are competing to get their attention against Facebook messages, text messages, hundreds of emails and other people also trying to cold call them.

Having said this, one recipe we found very effective was from the authors of MADE to STICK – Chip Heath and Dan Heath. Their Success Model requires your message to be simple, have something unexpected, have something concrete, have something credible, have something emotional and have a story.

If you can design your cold calling scripts using the above formula, your conversion rate on voice messages will dramatically increase.

What we've discovered in making thousands of cold calls, is that your story should have nothing to do with you directly. It should be about a big idea that you have. A problem you want to solve. A big idea or a problem that if you solved it, would excite you.

The next step to this is that you need to be persistent – which means if you don't hear back, you need to keep calling back. Consistently I have discovered after the 3rd call that someone responds with a date/time to meet or they simply decline the meeting.

Be prepared to take objections and think about how to turn them into a follow up reason for calling.

Call early in the morning before the executive assistant comes to the office to screen the calls or call after 5:30 pm when most assistants have left the office. Many executives come in early or stay late.

In the next chapter, I want to show you how to write effective emails to "cold" prospects. These are folks who have never heard from you.

CHAPTER 3:

Email

Chapter 3:

Email – How to send cold emails to prospects and get a high conversion rate when competing with hundreds of other emails

"Email has an ability many channels don't: creating valuable, personal touches – at scale." – David Newman

In the year 2000, I left Canada's largest telecommunications company – Bell Canada - and I started my own business. I thought the place where I would have the biggest leverage (and where I could bring some immediate value) would be the technology and the telecommunications industry. So, I put together a list of my top 500 prospective customers using different websites and started to email them. Shortly after sending each individual an email, a person called Doug Cummings agreeing to meet with me.

Doug was a Vice President at a company called BCE Emerges – a division of Bell Canada. In our meeting, Doug and I hit it off well and he introduced me to a friend of his – Ross Pellizzari. Ross at the time was the Vice President of Sales at Cisco Systems and shortly after our initial conversation, Cisco Systems became a client of mine. Over the following years, I started to grow my relationship with Doug and he took me into the companies that he started to work for. My job was simple – leverage my skill sets to help his sales teams get access to new leads and markets.

As our lead generation business started to grow, we strategically decided to focus on mastering the art of email.

This was at a time where everyone wanted to leverage social media and every other tool under the sun. But, we soon realized that email is the one application that everyone keeps using. So, mastering the art of email was a strategic decision we decided to make early on. We decided that once we could capture someone's attention on email, we could then connect with them on other social media platforms (such as LinkedIn) and create our "multi-touch" lead-nourishing programs. This model of thinking has been really effective for us.

Today, I get hundreds of cold emails where people want to sell me something and even when I express interest, most vendors have no clue how to connect with me on other platforms and provide me with content that would be relevant to my situation and related to their product/service.

Here is a typical example of cold email communication that I receive:

Hi,

Hope you are doing well.

We will help you by putting you on the first page of google.

Let me know if you are interested and I'll email you some of our services and associated prices.

Kind Regards,
Sales Person

There are several challenges with this kind of tactic.

First, imagine if I went to a bar and saw a beautiful lady sitting by herself at the bar. This is someone whom I haven't met before. What do you think my chances are of approaching her and asking her to leave the bar with me?

It's probably zero.

The problem with sending emails to cold contacts (people you don't know) and asking for a direct sale — "let me know if you are interested" is that most people will reject you. You will instantly increase the cost of making a sale because you will see a much higher rejection rate than normal.

One must keep in mind that the exchange of money is a demonstration of trust and no professional organization that I know, asks for the order without a real and authentic relationship being present between the vendor and the customer.

The second challenge with the above email is that you are only making one request. And for this to work, I, as a prospective customer, need to be looking for Search Engine Optimization (SEO) services and should have money set aside for online activities. And I can tell you the probability of finding me at the exact time that I need SEO services is pretty low. An alternative to making one request is to add a second request.

An alternative model to writing emails to cold contacts is as follows:

Hi Taimour,

As per introduction, my name is (your name) and I'm contacting you because I'm sure you've been noticed compared to 10 years ago, how the cost and time in identifying new customers has dramatically increased.

My customers constantly tell me the emotional pressure this causes (not to mention the additional hours we have to work per week is huge).

My organization (Name of Your Company) has recently invented new techniques that will instantly put your services on the top of Google searches. This will immediately translate into new exposure and revenue for your company.

Having looked at your website, I would love to schedule a 7-minute discovery call to show you some of our techniques and how they can impact your revenues within the next 10 days. Would you have some time next Tuesday afternoon?

Sincerely,
Your Name

PS - Next month we are introducing our new Twitter and Facebook lead generation framework. We believe implementing this simple-to-use program will boost your social media sales by 10%. Would you like to sign up for the introductory program? Three seats are remaining.

What makes the above cold email much more effective is that it's personalized. It talks about the "emotions" I'm dealing with when it comes to my challenges. It is relevant to the target audience. It is about them. It shows me that someone has researched me and my industry. You are telling me that you have something new. You are putting measurable numbers to your email and finally, you have made a second offer – a new Twitter and Facebook program.

In the next chapter, I want to show you how starting 'a noble cause project' instantly changes the number of people you can speak to and will change your career and life forever.

CHAPTER 4:

How to Leverage Noble Cause Projects

Chapter 4:

How to Leverage a Noble Cause Project to Impact Your Target Community

"What is the use of living, if it be not to strive for noble causes and to make this muddled world a better place for those who will live in it after we are gone?" — Winston Churchill

Sometime in 2007, I learned that I had become bored running my lead generation business. I was no longer inspired by helping another Fortune 500 company hit its revenue targets. It was just too boring. At the same time, one of my clients (Cisco Systems) wanted me to take a look at a key market for them – Healthcare. They were interested in doing something different and unique and what caused this conversation was a successful project they had done with David Suzuki called One Million Acts of Green.

Together with Cisco and my partner in healthcare (Wayne Mills – now former CIO of Trillium Hospital) we formed something that became One Million Acts of Person Centered Health.

The idea was to recognize that "I" as an individual am responsible for my health, and when I take ownership of that, I can transform the healthcare system. We had documentation and case studies showing that any transformation to the current health care system had limited effects and the only way for the system to transform was to get people to see that they are the ones who can be responsible for the state of their health.

Armed with this story, Wayne reached out to Hon. Elinor Caplan (now the former Minister of Health – Provincially and Federally) and got her involved in participating in our movement.

Once we had the story and a core team, we needed a platform that would allow us to scale and reach out to any executive in the world that we could get hold of. So, we decided to approach Cisco Systems and ask them to become our sponsor and allow us to leverage their telepresence technology. This technology allowed us to connect from Cisco Systems Canada to any of Cisco's offices around the world. The technology (for its time) was superb. It gave us video and voice capability that no other technology could give us.

Two years later, we had regular global events at Cisco Systems connecting patients and the youth with hospital CEOs. Our mission was to have our guests (patients and youth) give advice to hospital CEOs about the system, communications and what was missing in the current system. And all of this was achieved with someone like Elinor Caplan sitting beside me.

Global roundtable on One Million Acts of Person-Centered-Health with Minister of Health and executives from various healthcare organizations.

What we discovered was patients had unique data and insights that no one else seemed to have access to. They could talk about how their lives were being impacted by government and hospital policies.

After we completed our two-year journey and built a vibrant community, we handed One Million Acts of Person-Centered Health to Ontario Healthcare Association (OHA) – the largest healthcare association in North America. This, for me, resulted in several speaking opportunities and a number of organizations connected with me to pitch me their big ideas/products/services and ask me to engage with their organizations.

Having experience with building a global platform, I approached Ted Maulucci – Chief Information Officer at Tridel (Canada's largest condominium developer). My ask – can we start something called One Million Acts of Innovation and help put Canada on the world map?

Ted had a lot of questions about who I was, why I was approaching him and what were my true intentions. Given he didn't know me well (at first) he was hesitant in the beginning and as one meeting led to another, he eventually started to warm up to the idea that we could create a platform to help raise Canada's innovation rankings globally.

Our first session had less than ten people. Our second session had over fifteen. Our launch party had over ninety registered guests.

Our second session together

Our launch event – with over ninety senior executives

Executives from IBM connecting with students at our launch party.

Executives from government connecting with the community.

Our media exposure.

During the launch period, I was participating in a leadership program and that's where I met John King – our classroom leader. John had something unique about him. He was an inspiring speaker and a very well-spoken gentleman. One of his unique abilities was to hear things that were playing in a person's subconsciously mind and a natural gift to coach people. Shortly after my leadership course ended, I scheduled a call with John and told him about myself and what we were trying to accomplish with One Million Acts of Innovation and asked John if he could find a way to participate with us.

John King and Taimour Zaman

Together, we started to develop One Million Acts of Innovation into a global not-for-profit organization with multiple stakeholders in various countries.

Through One Million Acts of Innovation, my network connected me with folks such as Steve Wozniak, Margaret Atwood, executives at Facebook, Canada's top chief marketing officers, people from various media and publications.

Steve Wozniak and Taimour Zaman

Margaret Atwood and Taimour Zaman

Our big pitch day to executives at Facebook to get engaged
in One Million Acts of Innovation

As we started to grow One Million Acts of Innovation, we realized that giving power to our community would be what is required to expand and scale this program and our job was to create an environment for the connections and the empowerments to occur. John King called this an act of leadership instead of an act of management.

These pictures are from an evening event we had in order to co-create the future with stakeholders and invite them to participate and to lead their versions of One Million Acts of Innovation. What is unique about this model is that we didn't create an organizational strategy by ourselves, but rather co-created with a lot of stakeholders being at the table.

The evening was long and there were a lot of negotiations to be had. But I'm convinced if you are an expert facilitator (and fantastic listener) that this model will beat any conventional strategic planning model.

So, as we started to ask members how they would like to create their own platforms and different people came into the program and started their own adventures.

Rob Daleman (Marketing leader at Avaya) teaching students the art of marketing in today's complicated world.

As the platform started to grow, so did the issues surrounding innovation. One challenge we bumped into was when some of our students couldn't participate in "meaningful" co-op programs in schools because universities and colleges (at that time) wanted to have a stake in the intellectual property a company was developing. One of our efforts then became connecting academia to business and trying to resolve this issue so that companies wouldn't feel threatened inviting students to participate in strategic projects with them. Going to work on solving these new challenges gave us reasons to contact new people and/or be referred to new people.

Deans and Associate Deans of a few universities that we were trying to convince to give up the right to ownership of intellectual property.

This caused our movement to grow faster. Our sessions were now completely booked and it was hard to find a seat in any of our packed conference rooms.

As we started to grow, requests for speaking opportunities flourished. I remember a time where our biggest complaint was that we didn't have enough time to speak at all of them.

My closing keynote speech at University of Toronto

As we transferred authority from the leadership team directly to our members, the platform started to grow. Someone at Royal Bank of Canada (Canada's largest bank) wanted us to have an event with them to get millennials to come and talk about innovation.

Facilitating a conversation at Canada's largest bank about how to engage millennials

These activities led to an abundance of volunteers and activities. Avaya (one of our sponsors) started a program to leverage our youth and provide insights into their base of customers who were responsible for customer service departments.

Rob Daleman and me

What injected energy into our movement (from my perspective) was the students. They had this powerful energy about them. They all wanted a winning Canada on the global stage and once we got them engaged in various schools, the number of initiatives we started with them started to grow.

Students from Humber College waiting for my arrival

Once we started to see how students had a unique viral effect, we decided to leverage them and have them pitch the innovation story. We started case competitions where students would take someone's business challenge and work on it with a team of peers and give you some actionable ideas and insights.

A group of students at our pitch session, giving solutions to business executives.

As requests for speaking opportunities came to us, we started to ask our members to participate on our behalf and this caused the entire community to get engaged with us.

Once I started to get exposure for building a global platform, organizations from different places started to contact me asking for assistance in helping them launch their innovation labs and go to market strategies.

Dan Ruby from a region outside Toronto called me to talk to me about helping him build the Vaughn Innovation Center. This caused me to connect to some of the folks within my network and enabled him to connect me to some of the people within his network.

Muskoka Technology Association

Small associations from other places started to connect with us trying to figure out how to bring acts of innovation and technology into their communities.

However, the big project came when Capgemini (a leading technology consulting firm) called me from New York and wanted to hire me to start their movement. Together, we launched One Million Acts of Payments. The goal was to cause new acts of innovation in the payment industry by connecting different communities. We connected payment executives in developing countries to share best practices, ideas, projects, etc. with developed countries. We connected millennials to payment executives in different countries and exchanged ideas and strategies.

One Million Acts of Payments

Global session at Cisco Systems connecting payment executives

And using the same framework, our membership started to grow – Fast!

We then started to get calls from payment associations inviting our teams and students to come in and share our experiences at their big events.

Then one day, Toronto elected a new mayor: Rob Ford. Ford's election campaign was all about creating a lean government, and, once he got elected, he needed to cut over $500 million in city expenses. His big idea turned out to be to close down one in four libraries, lay off sixteen percent of the police, and nine percent of Toronto's Transit Commission. This caused a few of our students from one of our platforms to connect with other students in other platforms and create their own engagement opportunities.

Their big idea was to convince artists to go to city hall with a campaign called, "If you ask a different question, you should get a different answer."

A picture of Aaron (one of our students) talking to an art gallery owner

The game plan didn't end there. Students started to talk to others about their noble- cause projects. This gave them an environment in which to flourish and caused One Million Acts of Innovation to go viral.

What I discovered about Hyper Growth individuals and companies, is that you need to have a massively transformative statement. A statement that creates a big game, a game bigger than you, something that is inspiring and is authentic to you on a personal level, something that makes the hair on the back of your neck stand up. In the context of One Million Acts of Innovation, the game is about raising Canada's Innovation ranking by creating meaningful change in the world.

What I also discovered is building global movements requires character, integrity and the ability to be with the unknown. From many of the folks who have tried to copy what I do and how I do it, I discovered building a global platform requires a certain amount of courage and to be comfortable with the unknown. And in my follow-up book titled "Creating Global Movements that Matter," I talked about the need for being authentic to yourself. The challenge facing most folks trying to copy my ideas and platforms is that the cause and growth of these movements require a high degree of authenticity and character.

In the next chapter, I want to show you how to leverage social media to put fuel into your activities and how to build a large followers' list (like Twitter). This will create a certain brand authority and will support you in getting in front of anyone.

CHAPTER 5:

New Ways to Use Social

Chapter 5:

New Ways to Use Social Media to Access Anyone

"Social media is the ultimate equalizer. It gives a voice and a platform to anyone willing to engage" – Amy Jo Martin

For the past few years, I've been teaching advanced digital marketing & lead generation strategies to leading social media experts & their clients at the University of Ontario Institute of Technology. I've interviewed dozens of authors and experts. I've read all of the books and tested almost everything that I heard could work.

Here is a framework that you must apply before you think about which platform you want to use.

FIRST, truly understand who is the customer you want to go after and why.

SECOND, identify which platforms your customers use. Are they on LinkedIn? YouTube? Twitter? Facebook?

THIRD, join groups that your customers, potential partners or investors are located in and survey them (before you create content or sales pitches) and learn what your customer cares about. This could be a formal survey using something like Survey Monkey, but it might more likely be simply getting engaged with each community and asking questions and being authentic about learning about their needs, desires, aspirations, etc.

FOURTH, inquire about and link your unique value proposition and strengths to their challenges and aspirations.

FIFTH, create your own online groups on platforms your customers participate on. For instance, if they are on Facebook and LinkedIn, then create your own groups on Facebook and LinkedIn.

SIXTH, create profiles that are equivalent to your customers' job titles. If you are selling to Chief Information Officers, then make sure your job title is a Chief Information Officer, or that you engage with a Chief Information Officer to be the primary liaison with this group. This enables a peer-to-peer conversation vs. a vendor to customer conversation.

Next, take your contacts from one of the platforms, (Example: LinkedIn), and connect with them through another platform, (Example: Facebook.)

Here is a sample template you can use to send them a note:

> *"Hi First Name, I came across your profile here and thought it would help to reach out! I'm the founder of (Your Company Name). Maybe we can benefit from being connected here. Thanks!"*

Next figure out how many meetings with prospects you need to have in order to reach your revenue targets.

Assuming you need 10 new clients a month, at a 10% close rate, you'll need to generate 100 appointments per month.

Don't worry about which platform is the most popular. There will always be the most popular platform for today and another upcoming platform that you should consider participating in, in the future. The rule of thumb is that you don't have to be everywhere. Pick one platform and generate a lead. Then generate another lead and another. I promise you, generating leads or meetings will require a fair amount of creative thinking and time dedication. Once you are reliably producing solid leads, then move into another platform and continue the process.

Here is how I helped a real estate agent get instant leads via Twitter and Facebook in about 4 minutes. **https://www.youtube.com/watch?v=bRyw39mUtF0**

Once you've made a connection, create a follow-through plan. This is where a lot of sales reps and entrepreneurs fail.

They almost never have a follow-through plan. Put a different way, if I meet you today and want to sell you what I have, you may (for whatever reason) may not be ready to buy anything from me. That's why it's important for me to have a pre-built system that I can use to keep following up with you 6-12 months from now.

And, the best follow through program is what I call a *Multi-Touch Campaign Lead Nurturing Program*.

After the first call (regardless of whether you buy something from me or not), I need to come up with an attractive offer (sometimes referred to as a lead magnet). I need to send you 2-3 messages with valuable content and a lead magnet.

And after every 3rd or 4th message, I should set up another call. Now, once you've discovered how to take one contact and turn it into a lead, you can now look at digital agencies, artificial intelligence tools, etc. to increase your followers.

Here are some sample messages you can use:

"Hi (Name of Customer/Partner/Investor),

I came across your profile on LinkedIn and felt you and I have a few things in common. I would love to connect with you for networking purposes. Let me know if you would like to connect.

Sincerely,
Your Name"

Once they connected with you, a follow-up message could be:

"Hi (Name of Customer/Partner/Investor),

I came across a report about (which you think will be of interest to them and relates to your services) and I thought of you. There are some unique insights that I believe could impact your organization. I thought you could benefit from taking a quick read.

Your Name"

A week after, a follow-up note could be:

> "Hi (Name of Customer/Partner/Investor),
>
> There is a fantastic conversation happening in (Your Group Name) and we thought it would be great to hear your voice. Provide link to the discussion here.
>
> Let us know what you think. Thanks!
>
> Your Name"

And finally, to ask for the sales call:

> "Hi (Name of Customer/Partner/Investor),
>
> You and I have many areas of common interest, including sharing various online groups. Would it be possible for us to schedule a discovery call to see how we could help each other out? I truly enjoy learning how I could be of service to others and would love to learn more about you.
>
> Would you be free for a call sometime next Wednesday afternoon?
>
> Your Name"

Two weeks after your initial communication, send a follow-up note.

Sample template:

> "Hey (Name of Customer/Partner/Investor), Just following up on the last message I sent you. I would like to get a call set up if you're open to it. Let me know!
>
> Your Name"

Message on LinkedIn group would say:

> "Hey (Name of Customer/Partner/Investor), I saw that we're both connected to (someone common) and I would love to connect. Let me know if we could schedule a call for next Wednesday afternoon.
>
> Your Name"

Next – let's get in front of people you haven't connected to for a while:

Look at your existing contacts that you've been trying to get in front of for a while on your platforms such as LinkedIn and use this approach.

"Hey (Name of Customer/Partner/Investor), I was going through my contacts and noticed your profile. It's been a while since we connected. I would love to do a catch-up call. Would you be free next Wednesday afternoon? I'm looking forward to re-connecting with you. Your name"

Another option is to come up with a hook (sometimes referred to as an Ethical Bribe) for connecting with people you want to get in front of.

Here is a sample:

"Hey Name of Customer/Partner/Investor,

We've been connected here for a while and I thought you might be interested in a new book that I'm writing. It's all about how (Customer/Partner/Investor) can benefit from (a product/service you offer). May I have your permission to talk to you about it? Let me know how you would prefer us to connect.

Thanks,
Your name"

Three weeks later, send them the following message:

Hi (Name of Customer/Partner/Investor), Just wanted to follow up on the book I sent you a few weeks ago. My gut tells me some of the ideas mentioned could be applicable to some of your immediate priorities. Can I jump into a call and answer some questions you may have for me? Let me know if next Wednesday works for you? Thanks! Your Name

The key to getting in front of anyone today lies in the follow-through process that you create. If you don't have a multi-touch follow-through system, it will be harder for you to get in front of the people you want to meet and much harder to get people to remember you when they need your services.

In the next chapter, I want to show you how to instantly access groups of customers or investors. The insights discussed in the next chapter will surely help you when you need instant access to various communities.

CHAPTER 6:

How to access investors and customers?

Chapter 6:

How to instantly access a group of investors and customers?

"Almost overnight, the Internet's gone from a technical wonder to a business must" – Bill Schrader, businessman

You may be in a position where you need to attract a group of customers and/or investors – quickly. I remember when I was co-building Canada's Next Digital Executive Challenge, I needed to engage with a community of digital experts fairly quickly and without any budget.

In this case, I simply didn't have the ten years required to start a successful business. I needed a platform that had instant traffic and was demonstrating revenues.

Here is a step-by-step plan that could give you a group of customers/investors quickly.

STEP 1

Who do you want to serve and why? Identify your top 100 list of customers. The clearer you are, the shorter your sales cycles and the quicker and bigger your results will be.

STEP 2

Identify your list of assets; who do you know? What books have you read? What methodologies have you learned? What experiences have you gained in your career? What social media / digital platforms do you know to use?

STEP 3

Identify a few hooks (ethical bribes) that you can use in creating a mailing list or giving your prospects/investors an incentive to sign up for whatever you are offering.

STEP 4

Identify who has a list of your customers. This could be publications, conference producers, podcast and radio producers, etc.

STEP 5

Identify who your competitors are, as well as what are your customers'/investors' alternative options.

STEP 6

Identify sources of traffic online or within your network and survey your prospective customers/investors.

My favorite survey tool is picking up the telephone and booking a time to ask them a lot of questions. If you want to use online tools, I highly recommend using phrases such as,

"Please Help Me" … and ask your audience what you are looking for.

While surveying customers or investors, I look for an understanding of their needs, fears, challenges and what they are trying to accomplish. What's critical is that when you want to translate their needs and figure out how your products/services/ideas can support them, make sure to use their words/phrases instead of your interpretation of the survey results. What often gets in the way of translating surveys into successful products/services/ideas/etc. is how we collect data. Often when we are listening to prospects we listen as if we know more than them and/or use online surveys which rob us from truly understanding the emotions they are experiencing and/or collecting enough data to make a meaningful decision.

Through years of surveying folks, what I've discovered is if I can articulate their problem better than they can, I am instantly seen as an expert who can fix their problems (and the reality is that I'm not an expert; but, rather I was just listening deeply when interviewing folks). Once I finish my surveys, I try to give something of value to my contact as something they can use to help them move to the next step of their journey.

In my surveys, I always include a question like, "If you can ask me any question about x what would that question be?"

This allows me to get a deep understanding of what my ideal customer/investor is looking for. At the end of my surveys, I'm always looking for patterns.

And I always suggest ending your surveys with an ethical bribe such as, "I will provide answers to your questions in a future webinar/newsletter/etc. Please enter your name and email below to get on the announcement list."

STEP 7

When conducting surveys, here are the general categories that I like to ask people about:

Trends: What is the next big trend in (your industry) and why?

People and Culture: What should people and organizations be thinking about that they may not be thinking about? What are the biggest fears, frustrations or challenges facing corporations looking to adopt (your solution)? Why aren't your desires happening naturally? How would you assemble the best team in this industry?

Technology and User Interfaces: What is the process you use in mapping out the customer experience and trigger points to better design the user interface and be relevant to the end-user customer?

When interviewing the community, you want to serve, and listen deeply for the emotions that are at play. Listen for fears and frustrations. Listen for hopes and aspirations.

Listen for what they are hungry to buy and not for what you are hungry to sell.

Once I've conducted my surveys, I want to create a story that engages the right people. I want to make sure the data I've collected has been incorporated. And if I'm going to propose an idea, I want to make sure it's simple to understand and engages people with into what the project is about and I want to make sure I have removed any fear anyone may have.

Once you've conducted your research, you want to pick a niche. This is a counter-intuitive step; but it is a fundamental step that differentiates you, gets you to create relevant content and dramatically increases your revenues and reduces your sales cycle times.

When we were in the process of building 8 billion acts of innovations we could have made it about general innovation; but, instead we decided to focus on artificial intelligence (AI).

Our tagline became: Where artificial intelligence meets human creativity.

We knew that the growth of artificial intelligence (AI) would cause incredible employment opportunities worldwide. The work we did (combined with our team's experiences) gave us access to senior politicians, media organizations and CEOs across any region. With a focus on AI and not just innovation, we are crystal clear on who our audience is, who our potential sponsors are, etc.

In order to access anyone, most people start small. They want to put all of the jigsaw puzzles together. What I've discovered is that the opposite mindset works better.

The growth of One Million Acts of Innovation came primarily when we got into CBC – by accident. We were inundated with visits and phone calls from people wanting to get engaged.

STEP 8

Once you've conducted your initial survey, consider contacting television, newspapers, radio and podcast producers with "suggested content" for their upcoming episodes. Tell them about the research you've conducted and the findings you would like to share on their show.

Prior to walking into the media, you want to make sure you have a landing page (often referred to as a squeeze page) that captures your audiences' email and contact information.

Make sure you have a sign-up process that works and you have a well-thought-through follow-up process.

Step 9: You want to start to create content. What you want to know about writing good content is that it would be useful to have a customer persona. We name our customers' personas and we describe them in detail. What are their lives like, what are their working environments, etc.

"Persona of a Typical Prospect/Customer

A customer or prospect Persona "is a representation of the goals and behavior of a hypothesized group of users. In most cases, personas are synthesized from data collected from interviews with users. They are captured in one-to-two-page descriptions that include behavior patterns, goals, attitudes and environment, with a few fictional personal details to make the persona a realistic character. For each product, more than one persona is usually created, but one persona should always be the primary focus for the design."

"The objective of going through the exercise of creating a prospect/ customer personal is to be placing you in the mindset of the customers you are trying to serve.

The following questions will help you build the persona, intuit your customers' needs/pain points and build more effective and useful offerings.

The sample questions below may vary depending upon the type of product or service you are trying to sell, and may lead you to create other unique questions relevant to your target audience.

✓ What are his/her likes and dislikes?

✓ What are his behavior patterns?

✓ What social media does she use?

✓ What activities is he involved in?

✓ What are her needs and pain points?

✓ Who does he interact with and how?

✓ What technology devices does she use?

✓ What education and skills does he have?

✓ What market forces impact her and how?

✓ What physical locations does he frequent?

✓ What social changes may be impacting her?

✓ What does a typical day in his life look like?

✓ Where does she work and what is her job role?

✓ What is his attitude towards those around him?

✓ What does her future or desired future look like?

✓ What companies and brands does he interact with & how?

✓ What is her life like, with respect to friends, family, and colleagues?

✓ What are his goals in life personal growth, family, job-related?

✓ What online resources does she use (e.g., search engines, Wikipedia)?

✓ What are his concerns, needs, pain points, passions, motivations, aspirations?

✓ What is the age, gender, marital status, parental status, and income level for the persona?

"Creating a persona can be a powerful way to better understand your target customers." Source: Tom Vassos, Destination Innovation: Creative Mobile Marketing and Commerce Strategies"

In this stage, you want to keep in mind how people learn.

There are people who will learn if they can answer the question, Why do I need to know about this? There are people who will care more about, What is this all about? There are people who care more about how will this affect me and people who are just skeptical and think about what if this goes wrong. Knowing how to communicate your message to people who learn differently is vital and it's the key to getting in front of anyone.

From an exercise perspective, think about your current message and who you would like to get in front of and re-write your message to them using these different formats:

Why People – Why do they need to learn this? What's in it for them? Why is it important for them to learn what you are teaching them? What will they accomplish from learning it from you? What would they avoid if they learn it?

What People - are looking for you to teach them the theoretical – the history & science. Explain the history of how the system works.

How People need a recipe - They need specific action steps: step 1, step 2, step 3, etc.

What If People - need what if I go out and take action? They need to go out and take an action. At the end of the concept... here is what to go and do right now.

Show them how they will gain influence, lose influence, power affiliation and achievement – what will they get out of it? What will they avoid?

The key to what we do is to combine all of these when creating our content for our personas.

Once we have our persona and our content ready, we start to think about words. And we want to focus on words that are used to get money. Not all words are created equal. **EMOTIONAL VALUE WORDS are key in getting in front of anyone**. Value each work/phrase from $1 to $100. Which word is worth $100? Which is worth $1? What is the community you want to serve fearful of?

Here is an example I learned from one of my mentors – Eban Pegan. Eat the Pasta, Lose the pounds. Notice the emotional keywords used here?

STEP 9

Map out the customer's journey in purchasing something from you or investing with you. Think about how to start with educating them about new trends, risks/opportunities; getting the audience to evaluate you and then how to implement what you have to offer.

Here is an example of how we did it:

My friends and I are passive real estate investors and a division in my business builds and/or helps others commercialize robots. Together with my real estate group of investors we built what we believe is one of the largest databases of real estate investors in the world.

I then went to a real estate conference and met with George Ross (Donald Trump's former lawyer). I spent a few hours with him and got a chance to know him. I got his contact information and asked him if he would be willing to speak at my upcoming blog talk radio show that I was facilitating. George agreed. Later throughout the conference, I met other conference speakers and I did the same. Created an ongoing relationship.

I then had put together an army of keynote speakers (content) from participating in a real estate conference. I leveraged my database of investors and invited all of them to participate in a blog talk radio show to meet my keynote speakers. This gave me a chance to build a brand/relationship with them fairly fast. At the end of each show, I advertised a 7-day real estate seminar at our resort in Belize. This 7-day conference allowed me to build a stronger relationship with all of my database and once relationships had been established, I could talk about some of my personal experiences in investing in various projects and hopefully make a meaningful contribution to them.

This is an example of "mapping out the customer journey" prior to launching a product/service. A campaign is not a promotional activity for us. It's a strategic series of activities where we deliver new value in each part to our selected community. In this step, we are planning how the communication will get started and how the relationship will be built. We are creating the game plan and how the people we want to attract will hear about us and engage us.

STEP 10

I highly recommend writing 20-50 different articles, videos, etc. talking about the dangers, possibilities, and opportunities facing the community you want to serve. Use emotional and visual words because they convert much better. Create and give away free reports or case studies and make sure each blog is relevant to your specific target audience. For instance, if I were going to write a blog targeting government officials to get engaged into 8 Billion Acts of Innovation, I would talk about the fears and frustrations public servants have in communicating the value of AI to different classes of people and communities. Where you want to think from is what are the conversations, stories, etc. that are already going on in their minds that you can easily enter into.

Do they feel overwhelmed with multiple priorities? What is it? What are their top 3-5 desires?

STEP 11

Armed with good content and a database, you can start populating social media platforms like Facebook, LinkedIn, Twitter, etc. and start to identify your joint venture partners.

STEP 12

Brainstorm (typically with a group of friends or colleagues) about why people wouldn't want to buy from you or invest with your and identify all of their reasons to reject you. Once you've stacked up all of the reasons, come up with your counter reasons why they should buy from you/invest with you and look at where you can add this communication to your brochures, websites, etc.

For instance, I may not buy from you because you are a startup or your idea hasn't been proven. A counter offer would be – we have a new business model and/or we have partnered with a well-known organization like Deloitte/IBM/etc. to help deliver this solution. In this case, I'm leveraging well branded partners like Deloitte/IBM to bring a level of security to the project.

STEP 13

Brainstorm on the value proposition you offer to your customers, investors, etc. and come up with a minimum of 100 benefits. From our experience of doing this with hundreds of organizations, the real reasons (and unique value propositions) come up when groups have to think for hours and hours about what are the benefits of working with you are. This usually results into a 10-page document. By the time 100 benefits have been identified, you will discover concrete, measurable, tangible and experiential reasons why someone should buy from you and/or partner with you and/or invest in you. When looking at benefits, always go one or two levels deeper. Within every benefit there is another benefit. Ask yourself what is the next level of benefit from working with us? Once you have a list of 100 benefits, narrow it down to the top 5. But don't start your list with your top 5. Look into the future and ask yourself what is the cost of not doing business with you or partner with you or invest with you are.

Start with your 100 benefits/reasons why someone should buy from you, partner with you and/or invest with you and narrow it down. Come up with concrete language in what outcomes someone working with you can expect from you are. For some of our lead generation software, we explicitly say we will connect you to 20 prospective customers every day. It's important to use words that pay you money and convert fast, vs. any other word.

STEP 14

Reverse Engineer the sales/engagement process. Start from the end in mind – as if I just purchased something from you or invested with you or became your partner. Then work backwards. What must happen the day before and the before that and work your way to the first step that needs to take place.

STEP 15

The Art of Storytelling. What gets people engaged is the art of storytelling. Tell them the story of someone who has worked with you or bought from you or partnered with you and make sure that person is the hero of the story and not you. If you don't have a success story, then come up with another company's success story. Then demonstrate expertise by including statistics, quotes and use tons of emotional words. Tell them about the old world vs. the new world. When telling stories, you want to let your target community know what to pay attention to, how things might work and/or turn out and what the recent trends mean to them. Tell them about common mistakes and have a frequently asked questions sheet with you that will answer all of their subconscious questions. And if you did everything prior to this step correctly, then your content will be delivered differently compared to any of your competitors and/or alternative options that your target community has.

STEP 16

Always think through the next action step your audience must take and give them a quick start.

STEP 17

People buy from people. People rarely buy from companies. Every time I sold a major project to a large company like IBM, Microsoft, CGI, Siemens, Adobe, I learned what people were paying for, was me. Very rarely do people buy because of the brand. If you are willing to consider that people are looking for the authentic YOU and not a major brand, then you need to prepare a few stories about yourself. Stories that demonstrate you are a real human being and a corporate person.

When I am thinking about stories to share about myself, I share stories like my stories of struggle, the surprises I've discovered, my magic bullets, etc.

These stories make me human and not another sales person who is trying to get in front of anyone.

STEP 18

Think through Your Headlines

You and I participate in a digital economy where most communications are now communicated electronically. So, it's worth mastering the art of electronic communications if you want to get in front of anybody.

The first step in electronic communications whether in an email or website or whatever is to have a catchy headline. Consider that what sells newspapers and magazines are headlines. Not what is on page 16 or on page 47. So, if what sells a magazine or newspaper is a headline, then why spend most of your time in the content of your website or email?

Most people I know spend a lot of time thinking what they want to say in their emails or websites and miss the art of writing catchy headlines that capture the attention of the person they are trying to engage.

Your headline's number-one job is to grab the reader's attention. To accomplish this, your headline must either make a claim or promise, evoke an emotional response, or stir up curiosity.

Here are some techniques for writing email subject lines and/or website titles or blog headlines that will assist you in the art of getting in front of anyone.

Result (Benefit) Focus

How to Get [Result] [Quickly] [Without Risk]

Example: "How to Get Out of Debt In 30 Days"

Pain Focus

How To [Eliminate Specific Pain] [Without More Pain]

Example: "How to Lose 88 Pounds Without Going to The Gym

Action Focus

What to Do If [Specific Hot Button Situation]

Exercise: "What to Do If You Notice High Real Estate Prices

In Your Neighborhood"

Customer Focus

10 Mistakes Most [Describe What Your Customers Are doing] Make [In Situation] - And How to Avoid Them

Example: "10 Mistakes Most Investors Make When Investing in Real Estate"

In the next chapter, I will show you how some uncommon tools and strategies will help you get in front of anyone. I will also cover the power of referrals to aid in your success.

CHAPTER 7:

The Art of Referrals, Never-Seen-Before Technologies and Uncommon Tools and Strategies That Will Help You Get in Front of Anyone

Chapter 7:

The Art of Referrals, Never-Seen-Before Technologies and Uncommon Tools and Strategies That Will Help You Get in Front of Anyone

"Strategy is a pattern in a stream of decisions" —Henry Mintzberg

Have you ever been truly excited about something big in your life? Something that was worth sharing with the entire world? Chances are, you have. In my years of working with sales executives and entrepreneurs, what I discovered is that most people are happy and excited about joining a new company or starting a new company.

But often something happens to them in their experience of working with customers, colleagues, the boss or someone who kills their "mojo". That something is what I called a broken agreement and in most cases, it's subconscious. I know for me, there has been times where I felt nervous or resigned from doing something.

When the source of broken agreement is not discovered I am simply not myself. I am not living the life of a 5-year-old kid where I think everything in life is possible.

At the end of the day, you and I can read all kinds of strategies and tactics about how to get in front of anyone; but, the reality is that if you have lost your excitement, you will not take a sufficient level of action in order to be successful at getting in front of anyone nor anything else that you are not yet committed to.

The way to deal with broken agreements is to identify that it's playing in the background and to have a conversation with whomever the broken agreement is with – so that I (as a human being) am complete. And if the person you need to speak to has passed away, writing a letter to them could help make something complete for you.

Dave Logan and Steve Zaffron talk about it in their book "THE THREE LAWS OF PERFORMANCE" when they say people behave in the way life occurs for them.

Another technique to the art of getting in front of anyone is rejuvenation: physically, emotionally and intellectually. And any of these techniques will require discipline.

Constant actions and commitments require a big enough reason to do them. So, the question for me is always, what's the big 'Why' that will make all of the pain that I have to go through worth it? The reality is that I can't cheat life. There is no shortcut. So, if I'm going to play the game of life, then what's the game that will be worth all of the effort that is needed to go through it?

Once you are up and ready to get going, one common tool people use to get in front of anyone is asking for referrals.

Six degrees of separation is the idea that everyone and everything is six or fewer degrees of contact away, by way of introduction, from any other person in the world, so that a chain of a "friend of a friend" statements can be made to connect any two people in a maximum of six steps.

In 2010, I went to see my dear friend Ross Pellizzari, President and Managing Director of Avaya. I spoke to Ross about what we were doing with One Million Acts of Innovation and that our intention was to raise Canada's innovation rankings. Ross decided his organization should be a sponsor of our movement and introduced us to Heather Tulk, who was the Vice President of Marketing at Bell Canada (Canada's largest telecommunication company).

When I met Heather, I was clear she wouldn't be my actual customer and that someone below her in her organization would be the cheque-writer. The key in meeting Heather was to get her excited about what we were doing and invite her to introduce us to a few people below her as well as praise Ross and make the person responsible for the introduction the hero for introducing us to each other.

This powerful technique has two specific parts to it:

First, you need to design a message for your sponsor to hand it to your key prospect.

Second, you MUST ask your sponsor if they can introduce you to three people within their network who that would benefit from your idea/product/services. This will always cause your network to refer you to their contacts and relationships. As a thank you to Ross for his introduction, I introduced him to a friend of mine, Andy Aickeln. Andy had now become the new Vice President at HP's Software and Solutions when he received a call from me. Once I introduced Andy to Ross, Andy decided to introduce me to Charlie Atkinson – now Managing Director at HP Enterprises Canada. The lesson I've learned in growing my network to 120,000 trusted relationships around the world is that I should always be up to a big game and playing the game will always have people refer me to someone.

A proven platform, that eliminates years of building your own network is artificial intelligence. These technologies are designed to help you identify your next customer, your next investor, suggest content that you should be talking about to engage your audience. For me, I really started to see the power in these platforms when we started 8 Billion Acts of Innovation television show. After a year of running the show, we decided to synthesize various artificial intelligence platforms and start our own solution to help professionals write better content by enabling artificial intelligence to understand who is the audience we are trying to engage and allowing for the technology to rewrite or make suggestions on what to write to engage our audience.

For instance, if I want to engage a lawyer in Toronto Canada, in a project that requires him/her to volunteer for something, the artificial intelligent will scatter social media and other sources to tell me exactly what that lawyer is reading on, what his/her interests are and suggest keywords/phrases that I could use to instantly engage that lawyer.

This eliminates much of my writing/researching on how to engage my target audience.

The same technology can be applied for another lawyer in London England and will provide different suggestions (with a high level of accuracy using artificial intelligence) on what to say to engage that lawyer.

Here is a short video that shows you how this works: https://youtu.be/R33sZLchLb0

What I discovered from using this technology, is that there are always technologies that will make life a lot easier for me to use and that my job is to discover them, test them, and then give them to one of my assistants to run them for me.

The next uncommon technique that will help you get in front of anyone is getting good data and insights.

Try a company that you would like to go and see. Google their company name and put any of the following extensions to see what you will discover: "filetype", or ".xls", ".pdf", ".doc". Using this technique alone you will find information that your competitors may not have. When researching companies look at who reports to the CEO. Who are their suppliers? Look for jargon words they use and any line item from the CEO's speeches.

Research and come up with "original content" about a topic that you would like to have on television, radio, etc.

Once you've got your content prepared, find out the name of the producer of the show you want to be on and send them a note that says, "Suggested Content", and then write the topic you want to talk about.

Remember, each of these networks has air time, or newspaper space that they need to fill up. So as long as you give them content that is relevant to their show/topic of interest, they are likely to be interested in having you on the show. And when you are on their show, or writing a blog for them, you must remember that your entire content should be about them (and not you or your products/services). The art is in figuring out how your message, product/service will forward the goals of their show, newspaper article, etc. In the next chapter, FREE Bonuses, I would like to give you access to some of my tools, technologies, etc.

I'm sure you will enjoy using them.

Free Bonus:

Here are 7 critical tools we recommend using in enabling you to get in front of anyone: **www.access-group.ca**

About the Author:

Taimour Zaman is a lead generation consultant who mainly works for fast-moving companies like yours.

He is the founder of The Access Group (www.access-group.ca) and co-founder of **Eight (8) Billion Acts of Innovation (www.8billionactsofinnovation.com)**. Prior to this, he founded global organizations such as One Million Acts of Innovation, and Person-Centered Health. During the evening, he enjoys spending time with his family, investing in real estate, and investing in artificial intelligence companies, as well as writing books. His upcoming book is titled "Creating a Global Movement that Matters – How You Can Change the World with Passion, People, and Disruptive Technologies".

Taimour also teaches digital marketing & story telling at the University of Ontario Institute of Technology, is a frequent guest speaker at various conferences, and publishes courses at Udemy.

Taimour's Media Appearances

Recently, Taimour has been featured in the following articles:

- ISPIM – International Society for Professional Innovation Management: "Discover how Tesla is reinventing your company & your career without your participation"
- Huffington Post: "3 Changes in How to Acquire Today's Top Talent"
- The Green Sheet:" The very point of sale: Think big, go bold"
- Give Good: "Surrounding Yourself with Genius"
- University of Waterloo: "On Innovation"
- CBC Interview: "Interview about our Programs"
- IT World: "Error! Hyperlink reference not valid."
- CBC: "Tallying '1 million acts of innovation"
- Your Legacy: "Discover Taimour Zaman"
- Association of Career Professionals: "Careers of the Future"
- The Gilford Group: "Surviving, Competing & Prospering in the new age of the high Canadian Dollar"

Taimour's content

For years, Taimour has been known as the creative lead generation expert. He finally decided to own that role and be intentional about it. His mission is to help overwhelmed executives discover their passions, products, customers, and opportunities by designing creative out-of-the-box marketing and digital campaigns based on their core values and capabilities so that they enjoy a growth in sales and customers.

Taimour has been facilitating executive roundtables on topics around innovation, digital technologies and culture. His goal is to create insightful, relevant content that you can instantly put to work in your organization. His ultimate goal is to create a world where we are constantly creating what is next for each of us.

Taimour's biography

Taimour began his career at Packard Bell NEC and later moved to other technology companies like Dell Computers and Bell Canada. In the year 2000, he started a marketing agency called Access Group and helped technology and professional services organizations access new insights and relationships into their strategic markets. I did some work for global corporations such as IBM, Microsoft, CGI, Bell and many more.

In 2005, he found himself interested in leadership training and development and started his own journey in executive coaching and transformation of corporate cultures.

In 2008, Taimour and a few of his friends started a noble cause project called **One Million Acts of Innovation**. Today, that project has turned into a global not-for-profit designed to help create meaningful change in the world.

Taimour's family

Taimour & Anitra Persad were married in 2012 and live in Toronto, Ontario.

In his free time, he enjoys reading, photography, running, and practices martial arts.

Taimour's Contact Information

You can contact Taimour via email at taimour@access–group.ca

Resources to Connect to Your Customer in a New Ways:

The Access Group offers a number of resources to help you implement connecting to your customers in new ways: The training programs provides you with everything you need to implement the strategies and ideas in this book. When you join, you'll learn:

- How to design advisory boards correctly so that they can produce new customers and/or investors?

- The art of cold calling

- How to write email campaigns to cold prospects?

- How to start a noble-cause project?

- How to use social media to access anyone?

- The art of instantly accessing groups of customers or investors

- How to leverage various technologies to help you get in front of anyone

**You can connect with us at
The Access Group at www.access-group.ca
or call us at 416-629-7924**

Made in United States
North Haven, CT
24 July 2022